MEGA Puzzles

PIRATES

bookoli

How quickly can you match these pesky parrots into pairs? Get set, GO!

Answers on page 62

Help the crew find the secret treasure. Watch out for jagged rocks along the way!

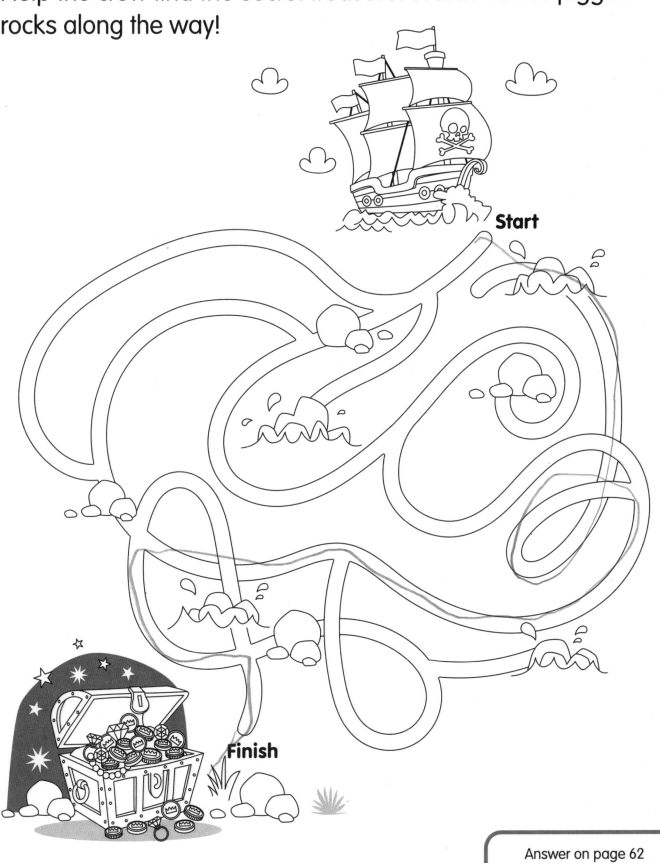

Start

Finish

Answer on page 62

These crews are battling it out to become the speediest ship at sea! Add up the numbers along each path. The highest total wins.

9

10

Answers on page 62

Can you spot all of these precious treasures in the big grid?

Gold
Jewels
Silver
Crown
Chest
Ruby

P	J	E	W	E	L	S	S
G	R	T	I	E	R	I	O
O	O	I	C	A	N	L	C
L	V	L	N	T	Q	V	R
D	P	R	S	C	U	E	O
B	Z	E	N	G	E	R	W
R	H	I	Z	R	U	B	Y
C	R	O	W	N	B	A	L

Answers on page 62

How many crocodiles can you spot lurking in the lagoon?

I can spot [6] crocodiles.

Answer on page 62

Match each fearsome pirate to their shadow.

Answers on page 62

Connect the dots to reveal a creature lurking in the deep.

Answer on page 62

Land ahoy! Guide the ship safely through the storm and to the island.

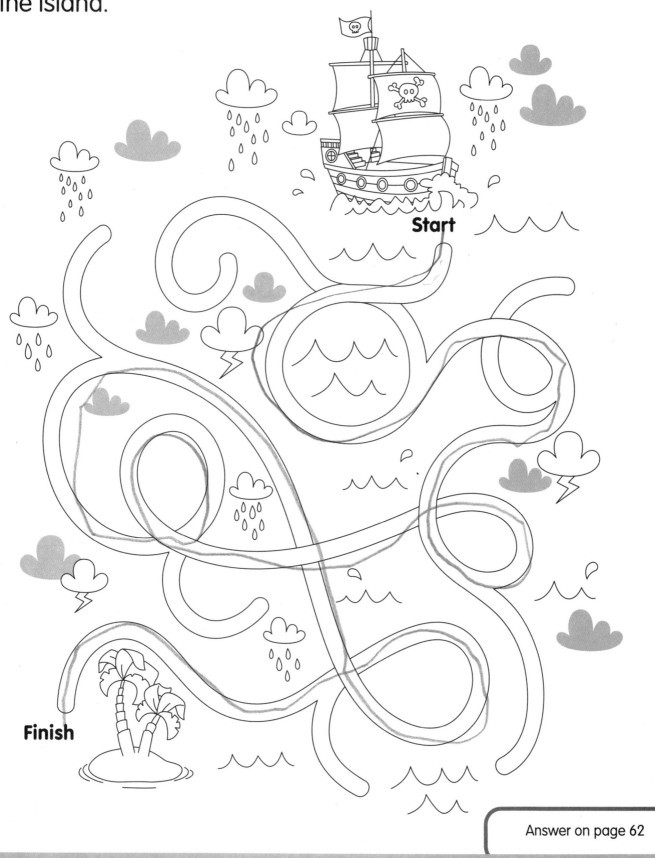

Start

Finish

Answer on page 62

A pirate never forgets! Test your memory by looking at this picture for one minute. Cover it up and answer the questions.

Can you remember...

1. How many treasure chests there are? .... 2 ....

2. What is on the pirate flag? .... skull ....

3. What animal is lurking in the cave? .... monster ....

4. How many pirate hats there are? .... 1 ....

Answers on page 62

So many swords! How many can you count here?

I can count ⌊16⌋ swords.

Answer on page 62

Spot the odd treasure out in each row.

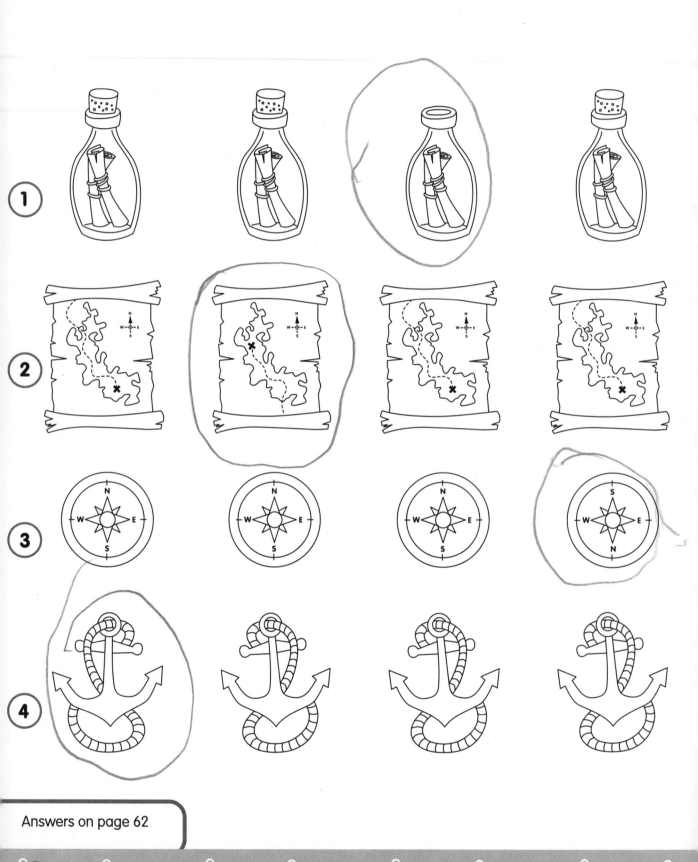

The captain's parrot has escaped again!
Use the clues to spot him below.

1. He has an eye-patch.
2. He has one sword.
3. He has two tail feathers.

Answer on page 62

Pirates love counting up their silver! Can you complete all of the sums below?

1  + = 8

2 + = 8

3 + = 9

4 + = 12

Answers on page 62

Thar, she blows! How many cannon balls can you count in the scene?

I can spot 4 cannon balls.

Answer on page 62

How many times can you spot the word AHOY in this grid? Words can go up, down and across.

A	H	O	Y	E	L	S	A
H	R	T	O	E	R	I	H
H	O	O	A	H	O	Y	L	O
Y	O	H	A	T	Q	V	Y
D	P	O	S	C	U	Y	O
B	Z	Y	N	G	E	O	W
R	A	H	O	Y	U	H	Y
C	E	J	W	N	B	A	L

Answer on page 62

It's time for a treasure hunt! Count up the coins along each path to find out who has collected the most booty.

6

7

5

Answer on page 62

Join the dots to complete the pirate flag and get ready to set sail!

Answer on page 62

Help this pirate reach the island by hopping on stepping-stones with even numbers: 2, 4 and 6. Quick, before the tide comes in!

Start

Finish

Answer on page 62

Adventure ahoy! Can you spot six differences between the pictures of this secret island?

Answers on page 62

Follow the directions to find out where the treasure is buried.

1. **North 6 squares**
2. **East 4 squares**
3. **South 2 squares**
4. **West 1 square**
5. **North 5 squares**
6. **East 3 squares**

Start

Now draw an X to mark the spot!

Answer on page 62

This captain is counting up his plunder. Work out the missing numbers in each tower of gold by adding together the numbers in the two bars below it.

a

9

5 4

1 2 2

b

14

8 6

2 3 3

c

14

9 5

4 2 3

Answers on page 63

Imagine you are about to set off on a voyage! Draw all the places you will visit on your map.

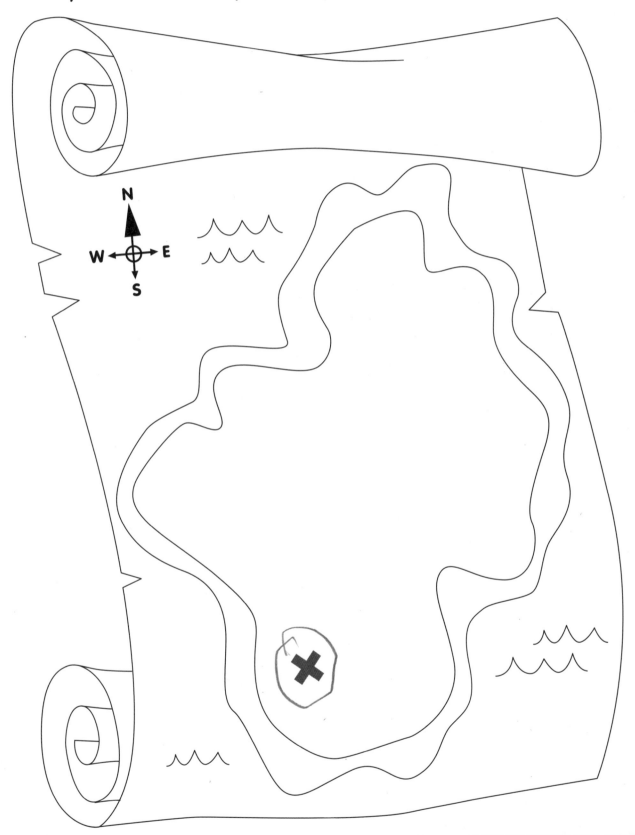

Double trouble! Can you spot six differences between these pictures of the terrible pirate twins?

Answers on page 63

This pirate is pulling his fiercest face! Can you spot him in the crowd?

Answer on page 63

Squawk! Follow the wiggly lines to match each pirate to his pet parrot.

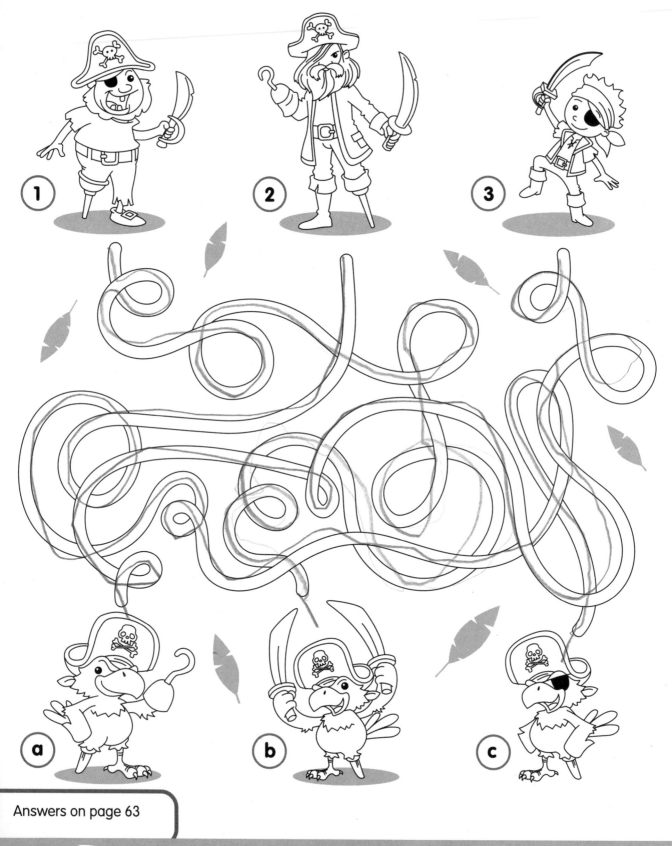

Answers on page 63

Draw in the missing jewel in each row.

1

2

3

4

5

Answers on page 63

Search the ship for the five objects from the panel.

Answers on page 63

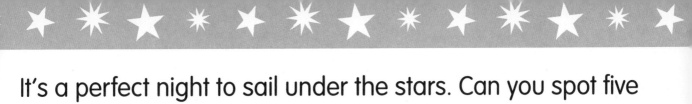

It's a perfect night to sail under the stars. Can you spot five differences between the pictures?

Answers on page 63

This pirate wants to join a crew, but a crew can only have 7 pirates. Count the pirates in each group to see which one she should join.

Answer on page 63

It's shipwreck sudoku! Draw in the missing objects.
Remember, each item can only appear once in each
row and column.

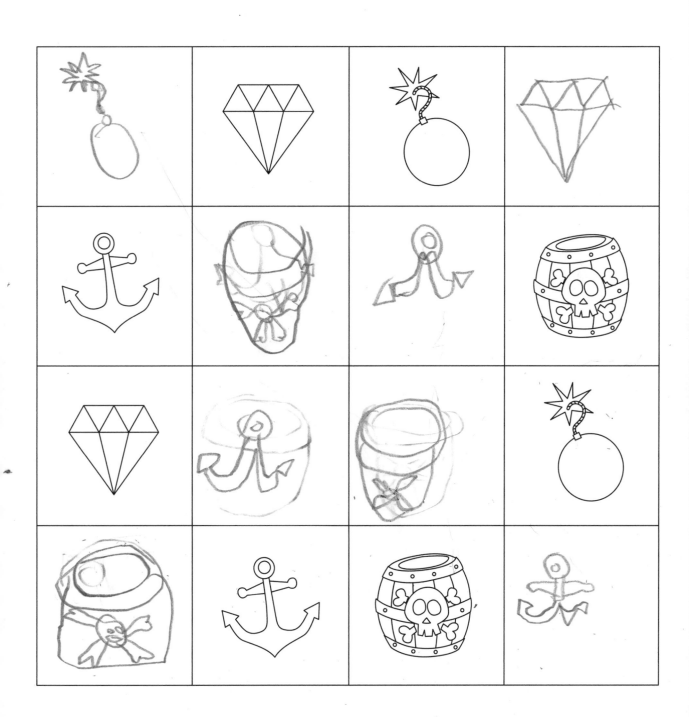

Answers on page 63

This fearless captain is searching for the legendary sea monster. Follow the directions to find the beasty.

Start

1. North 6 squares
2. West 1 square
3. North 3 squares
4. East 7 squares
5. South 1 square

Answer on page 63

Cross out the pirates that appear twice to reveal the famous Captain Crabby, master of the high seas.

Answer on page 63

How many of each object can you spot on the busy beach?

Answers on page 63

It's time for some sea shanties! Can you spot six differences between the pictures of this crooning crew?

Answers on page 63

Do you dare to join the pirates for a game of Skulls and Crossbones?

💀 You need 2 players for this game.

💀 Decide who will draw skulls and who will draw bones.

💀 Take it in turns to draw your picture in one of the squares.

💀 The first player to get three in a row (down, across or diagonally) is the winner.

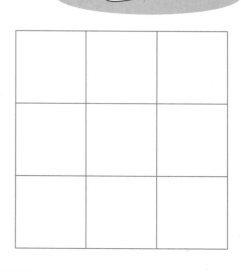

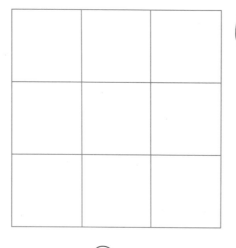

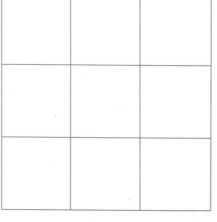

Best of three!

Count up the jolly roger flags on board this ship.

I can count ☐ flags.

Answer on page 63

Can you spot Captain Redbeard amongst these pirate impostors?

Can you find all these nautical words in the grid below?

Crow's nest
Booty
Deck
Sail
Mast
Plank

B	O	O	T	Y	E	F	E	N
L	E	I	I	E	F	C	O	O
C	R	O	W	S	N	E	S	T
N	B	D	N	D	M	R	N	N
O	P	R	K	C	U	I	P	M
I	S	C	A	S	A	I	L	M
Y	E	I	R	V	Y	U	A	A
D	P	B	K	I	D	S	N	S
C	R	S	A	I	A	T	K	T

Answers on page 63

Rise and shine! Which crewmate is missing something from his pirate get-up?

Answer on page 63

It's a pirate's life for me! Draw in the five missing things to make the top picture match the bottom picture.

Answers on page 63

One of the crew has been looting treasure. Use the clues to find the culprit and make him walk the plank!

1. He's wearing stripes.
2. He does not have a beard.
3. He has an eye-patch.

Answer on page 64

This rough and tough captain is a softie at heart! Connect the dots to reveal his cuddly companion.

Answer on page 64

Which close-up from this pirate's spyglass doesn't appear in the picture?

(a)
(b)
(c)
(d)

Answer on page 64

Anchors away! How many anchors can you count?

I can count ☐ anchors.

Answer on page 64

Can you match these slippery sea monsters into pairs?

Answers on page 64

Help the pirate climb up to the treasure by adding up the numbers under each square.

Answers on page 64

Pirates sail no matter the weather! Draw in the five missing things to make the pictures match.

Answers on page 64

This captain can't remember where he docked his ship!
Use the clues to help you find it.

1. It has three sails.
2. It has two portholes.
3. It doesn't have a skull sail.

Answer on page 64

How many message bottles can you spot in this sandy cove?

I can spot message bottles.

Answer on page 64

Draw lines to match each parrot to its shadow.

Answers on page 64

It's a busy day at the docks! Answer these questions before the ships sail away.

1. Which ship is the biggest? ....

2. Which ship is the smallest? ....

3. Which ship has the most sails? ....

Answers on page 64

Which path will lead the pirate to the treasure?

Answer on page 64

There are lots of pirates at this party. See if you can spot the following:

1. The smallest pirate.
2. The pirate with a hook for a hand.
3. The pirate with one tooth.

Answers on page 64

Which pirate is missing something from his treasure hoard?

Answer on page 64

Captain Cutlass is proud of his new portrait. Spot which painting is his by matching him to the picture.

Answers on page 64

Every crew member is important! Draw lines to connect each job to the correct pirate.

Chef   Cleaner   Navigator   Captain   Parrot tamer

1

2

3

4

5

Answers on page 64

This pirate needs your help breaking the code! Circle every other letter on the scroll to reveal the location of the treasure.

_ _ _ _ _ _

_ _ _ _ _ _ _

Answer on page 64

Match each close-up to a member of the crew.

Let's go on an adventure! Find a route across the sea.

Start

Croc Cave

Treasure Island

Palm Island

Mermaid Lagoon

Finish

What places did you go along the way?

_____ and _____

Answer on page 64

Answer Page

Page 2

Page 3
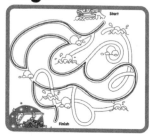

Page 4
Ship b wins.

Page 5
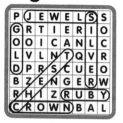

Page 6
There are 6 crocodiles.

Page 7
1e, 2c, 3d, 4a, 5b.

Page 8

Page 9

Page 10
1. 2 treasure chests
2. A skull and crossbones
3. An octopus
4. 1 pirate hat

Page 11
There are 17 swords.

Page 12

Page 13
Parrot 5 is the captain's pet.

Page 14
1. 8
2. 8
3. 9
4. 12

Page 15
There are 6 cannon balls.

Page 16
AHOY appears 9 times.

Page 17
Pirate 2 collected the most treasure.

Page 18

Page 19

Page 20

Page 21

Answer Page

Page 22

Page 24

Page 25
Pirate 9.

Page 26
1b, 2c, 3a.

Page 27

Page 28

Page 29

Page 30
She should join crew b.

Page 31

Page 32

Page 33

Page 34
1 crab, 2 shells, 6 coins,
3 rings and 2 bottles.

Page 35

Page 37
There are 6 flags.

Page 38
6 is Captain Redbeard.

Page 39

Page 40
5 is missing a buckle.

Page 41

Answer Page

Page 42

Page 43

Page 44

Item c doesn't appear.

Page 45

There are 19 anchors.

Page 46

Page 47

Page 48

Page 49

Page 50

There are 5 bottles.

Page 51

1d, 2b, 3c, 4a

Page 52

1. b
2. c
3. b

Page 53

Path c leads to the treasure.

Page 54

1.    2.

3.

Page 55

Pirate d is missing a jewel.

Page 56

The correct painting is d.

Page 57

1. Parrot tamer
2. Cleaner
3. Chef
4. Navigator
5. Captain

Page 58

The location is PALM ISLAND.

Page 59

1d, 2a, 3c, 4b.

Pages 60-61

You visited Croc Cave and Treasure Island on the way.